ODD NUMBERS

By CHARLES GHIGNA

Illustrations by MISA SABURI

Music by MARK OBLINGER

CANTATA
LEARNING

WWW.CANTATALEARNING.COM

CANTATA
LEARNING

Published by Cantata Learning
1710 Roe Crest Drive
North Mankato, MN 56003
www.cantatalearning.com

Library of Congress Cataloging-in-Publication Data
Names: Ghigna, Charles. | Saburi, Misa, illustrator. | Oblinger, Mark.
Title: Odd numbers / by Charles Ghigna ; illustrations by Misa Saburi ; music
  by Mark Oblinger.
Description: North Mankato, MN : Cantata Learning, [2018] | Series: Winter
  math | Audience: Age 3-8. | Audience: K to grade 3.
Identifiers: LCCN 2017007543 (print) | LCCN 2017017634 (ebook) | ISBN
  9781684100446 | ISBN 9781684100439 (hardcover : alk. paper)
Subjects: LCSH: Numbers, Natural--Juvenile literature. | Counting--Juvenile
  literature.
Classification: LCC QA141.3 (ebook) | LCC QA141.3 .G4834 2018 (print) | DDC
  512.7/2--dc23
LC record available at https://lccn.loc.gov/2017007543

Book design, Tim Palin Creative
Editorial direction, Flat Sole Studio
Executive musical production and direction, Elizabeth Draper
Music arranged and produced by Mark Oblinger

Printed in the United States of America in North Mankato, Minnesota.
072017   0367CGF17

ACCESS THE MUSIC!
SCAN CODE WITH MOBILE APP
CANTATALEARNING.COM

TIPS TO SUPPORT LITERACY AT HOME

WHY READING AND SINGING WITH YOUR CHILD IS SO IMPORTANT

Daily reading with your child leads to increased academic achievement. Music and songs, specifically rhyming songs, are a fun and easy way to build early literacy and language development. Music skills correlate significantly with both phonological awareness and reading development. Singing helps build vocabulary and speech development. And reading and appreciating music together is a wonderful way to strengthen your relationship.

READ AND SING EVERY DAY!

TIPS FOR USING CANTATA LEARNING BOOKS AND SONGS DURING YOUR DAILY STORY TIME

1. As you sing and read, point out the different words on the page that rhyme. Suggest other words that rhyme.

2. Memorize simple rhymes such as Itsy Bitsy Spider and sing them together. This encourages comprehension skills and early literacy skills.

3. Use the questions in the back of each book to guide your singing and storytelling.

4. Read the included sheet music with your child while you listen to the song. How do the music notes correlate to the words of the song?

5. Sing along on the go and at home. Access music by scanning the QR code on each Cantata book. You can also stream or download the music for free to your computer, smartphone, or mobile device.

Devoting time to daily reading shows that you are available for your child. Together, you are building language, literacy, and listening skills.

Have fun reading and singing!

Every number is either even or odd. How do you tell the difference? The children in the story see many wonderful things during the winter season. They have learned that if they **pair** these things up into groups of two and there is one left over, then they have an odd number.

Turn the page to learn how to tell if a number is odd. Remember to sing along!

Groups of numbers are everywhere.
Even numbers come in pairs.

Odd numbers mean one is left out.
Without a **partner** an odd's about.

1 tree stands in the middle of the room.
What a beautiful view!

Without a partner, it's all alone.
Yes, 1 is odd. It's true!

3 boots stomp through the snow!
Oh, look at them go!

Is 1 left over when you pair them up?
Yes! 3 is odd. Ho, ho!

5 cars speed around the track.
They are racing so fast!

Is 1 left over when you pair them up?
Yes! 5 is odd. Don't crash!

7 mittens keep hands so warm.
That's just what they're for!

Is 1 left over when you pair them up?
Yes! 7 is odd. Do more!

9 dogs pull a sled through snow.
Zip, zoom, off they go!

Is 1 left over when you pair them up?

Yes! 9 is odd. Now you know!

1, 3, 5, 7, or 9.

If you see numbers that end in

1, 3, 5, 7, or 9.

An odd number is your friend.

35 91

Now look for the odd numbers in front of you.

 89 52

27

Groups of numbers are everywhere.
Even numbers come in pairs.

Odd numbers mean one is left out.
Without a partner, an odd's about.

SONG LYRICS
Odd Numbers

Groups of numbers are everywhere.
Even numbers come in pairs.
Odd numbers mean one is left out.
Without a partner, an odd's about.

1 tree stands in the middle of the room.
What a beautiful view!
Without a partner, it's all alone.
Yes, 1 is odd. It's true!

3 boots stomp through the snow.
Oh, look at them go!
Is 1 left over when you pair them up?
Yes! 3 is odd. Ho, ho!

5 cars speed around the track.
They are racing so fast!
Is 1 left over when you pair them up?
Yes! 5 is odd. Don't crash!

7 mittens keep hands so warm.
That's just what they're for!
Is 1 left over when you pair them up?
Yes! 7 is odd. Do more!

9 dogs pull a sled through snow.
Zip, zoom, off they go!
Is 1 left over when you pair them up?
Yes! 9 is odd. Now you know!

1, 3, 5, 7, or 9.
If you see numbers that end in
1, 3, 5, 7, or 9.
An odd number is your friend.

Now look for the odd numbers in front of you.

Groups of numbers are everywhere.
Even numbers come in pairs.
Odd numbers mean one is left out.
Without a partner, an odd's about.

Odd Numbers

Slapstick Pop
Mark Oblinger

Intro/Outro

Groups of num-bers are eve-ry-where. E-ven num-bers come in pairs. Odd num-bers mean one is left out. With-out a part - ner, an odd's a - bout.

Verse

1. One tree stands in the mid-dle of the room. What a beau-ti-ful view! With-out a part - ner, it's all a-lone. Yes, one is odd. It's true!

Verse 2
3 boots stomp through the snow.
Oh, look at them go!
Is 1 left over when you pair them up?
Yes! 3 is odd. Ho, ho!

Verse 3
5 cars speed around the track.
They are racing so fast!
Is 1 left over when you pair them up?
Yes! 5 is odd. Don't crash!

Verse 4
7 mittens keep hands so warm.
That's just what they're for!
Is 1 left over when you pair them up?
Yes! 7 is odd. Do more!

Verse 5
9 dogs pull a sled through snow.
Zip, zoom, off they go!
Is 1 left over when you pair them up?
Yes! 9 is odd. Now you know!

Verse 6
1, 3, 5, 7, or 9.
If you see numbers that end in
1, 3, 5, 7, or 9.
An odd number is your friend.

Now look for the odd numbers in front of you.
[instrumental break]

Outro

23

GLOSSARY

pair—two like things

partner—one of a pair

GUIDED READING ACTIVITIES

1. What sort of activities do you enjoy during winter? Draw a picture of yourself doing one of these activities.

2. This song mentions a clue to know whether a number is odd. Remember what it is? Look back on pages 18 and 19. Then write down as many odd numbers as you can think of.

3. Listen to this song again. When you here a number sung, clap your hands that many times. So when you hear the number "one," clap your hands once.

TO LEARN MORE

Brinker, Spencer. *Odd or Even in a Monstrous Season*. New York: Bearport Publishing, 2015.

Ghinga, Charles, *Even Numbers*. North Mankato, MN: Cantata Learning, 2018.

Walters, Jennifer Marino. *Wonderful Winter*. Egremont, MA: Rocking Chair Kids, 2017.

Weakland, Mark. *Scooby Doo! An Even or Odd Mystery: The Case of the Oddzilla*. North Mankato, MN: Capstone: 2015.